MAMMOTHS AND MASTODONS

TITANS OF THE ICE AGE

MAMMOTHS

Abrams Books for Young Readers

New York

MASTODONS
AND

TITANS OF THE ICE AGE

Cheryl Bardoe

Published in association with The Field Museum, Chicago

Surprise in the Snow

Ten-year-old Kostia squinted through the snow that blows across northern Siberia even in May. He and his brother Edik had just loaded their reindeer sledge with firewood when they noticed an odd lump by the river. Kostia guessed it was an injured reindeer. But when the brothers drew closer, Kostia could hardly believe his eyes. The strange dead animal had no antlers—but it had a trunk like an elephant. Kostia and Edik poked at the animal and then hurried home.

Their father, Yuri, was troubled when he heard about the mysterious creature. Kostia's family is of the Nenets people, who live a nomadic life herding reindeer across the arctic tundra. Yuri believed the animal his sons saw came from the underworld below the Earth's surface—anything from underground could bring terrible luck. Yuri hiked to a sacred place on the tundra, marked by a pile of reindeer antlers. There he made an offering to the spirits and pondered what to do.

Sometimes a Nenets person would come across a mammoth tusk jutting from the ground and could transform a bad omen into good fortune by sharing the valuable ivory with others. Yuri decided to do the same with his sons' discovery. He had heard how others had found tusks, bones, and such, which attracted scientists from all over the world to the icy arctic. Yuri hiked 73 miles over four days to the nearest village to report the sighting of the creature.

Kostia and Edik's find was big. More than once-in-a-lifetime big. More than once-in-a-millennium

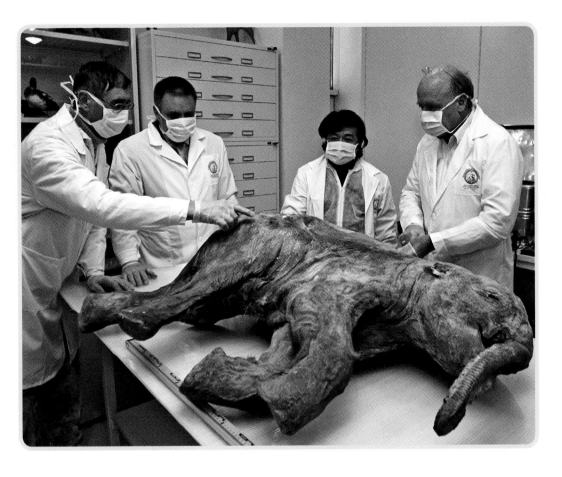

big. They had discovered a frozen baby woolly mammoth! People had discovered the bones of mammoths before. They had even found large parts of frozen mammoth bodies. Never had anyone found a mammoth—or any other extinct, prehistoric animal— that was completely whole and so well preserved. This baby mammoth died about 40,000 years before she was found in 2007. Yet wrinkles still creased her skin and taste buds dotted her tongue. Her eyeballs rested in their sockets, and her internal organs had retained nearly all their original shapes. Scientists call the baby mammoth Lyuba and study her in hopes of learning secrets from the past.

▲ More than 10,000 years ago, Columbian mammoths enjoyed water holes in North America. Scientists believe mammoths acted like elephants, in addition to looking like them.

Mammoths Are Extinct, but Their Story Isn't Over

Scientists have long figured that if a mammoth's skeleton looked like an elephant's, then it probably walked like an elephant. And if a mammoth's teeth looked like an elephant's, then it probably ate like an elephant. And if a mammoth walked and ate like an elephant, then it probably did other things like an elephant, too. Without physical, hold-in-your-hands evidence, however, these theories are just guesses about how mammoths may or may not have acted.

DID DINOSAURS AND MAMMOTHS LIVE AT THE SAME TIME?

Answer: No! Dinosaurs were a group of reptiles that included the largest animals ever to live on land, and they died out 65 million years ago. At that time, mammals—animals covered with fur that give birth to live young— were not much bigger than cats. Mammoths and mastodons were among the largest *mammals* ever to have lived on land. The first mastodons appeared around 25 million years ago, and the first mammoths appeared around 5 million years ago. Elephants appeared at the same time as mammoths. They were all still tromping around when modern humans appeared about 100,000 years ago.

"As a paleontologist, my job is to search the fossil record for clues to what mammoths did," says Dr. Daniel Fisher, a world-renowned mammoth expert and professor at the University of Michigan. For instance, scientists found dung in Lyuba's intestine. They know baby elephants nibble on poop to get bacteria into their stomachs to help digest leaves. Now they have proof mammoths did, too.

Enough clues have piled up to convince scientists that mammoths and their lesser-known cousins the mastodons did act a lot like elephants. Scientists' guesses were correct—they can study the living creatures to learn about the extinct ones. This is truly amazing because scientists know most long-lost animals only from their bones. Compare mammoths to amphicyonids, mammals that lived about 15 million years ago. Dr. Fisher helped unearth a set of five amphicyonid footprints, which had hardened into siltstone, on a school field trip when he was 14 years old. "This animal was as big as a bear," Dr. Fisher explains. "But no animal alive today is anything like it." As a result, scientists know little about how this animal ate, slept, and reared its young.

Having only bones to examine also means that scientists must guess at what most prehistoric creatures looked like alive, in the flesh. Discoveries like Lyuba show us the hulking muscles and shaggy fur that covered mammoth skeletons. They reveal that mammoth trunks worked like elephant trunks and that mammoths (like elephants) had thick, spongy tissue on the soles of their feet to help support their massive weight. Usually the soft parts of an animal's body rot after death, but a deep freeze puts the brakes on decay. Because woolly mammoths were enormous and lived in an arctic climate, they were the most likely animals to be preserved as prehistoric popsicles.

TREASURES FROM PERMAFROST

Near the Arctic Circle, the summer sun's rays often thaw only the top few inches of soil. A deeper layer of soil, called permafrost, may stay frozen for thousands of years. Massive woolly mammoths were more likely than smaller animals to induce a mudslide or crash through ice into rivers. There they could be blanketed by mud and frozen quickly after death.

◄ Except for the shaggy brown fur, this frozen woolly mammoth foot looks like an elephant foot. Broad feet spread the weight of these animals over a large area so that each step put less pressure on any square inch of ground than a lady's high-heeled shoe.

Scientists also learn about mammoths through clues left by humans. Our ancestors speared mammoths for supper and stacked their bones to build shelters from the wind. They painted mammoth pictures on caves and carved mammoth figurines from ivory (similar to art inspired by elephants).

With data from so many sources, scientists know more about mammoths and mastodons than about most other prehistoric creatures. Yet we don't know why these animals died out. Solving this mystery becomes even more urgent as elephants struggle to survive today.

Dr. Fisher hopes his research can help save elephants. "This is part of why I do this work," he says. "Part of me looks backward and tries to understand the past. And part of me looks around and tries to understand the animals of the present."

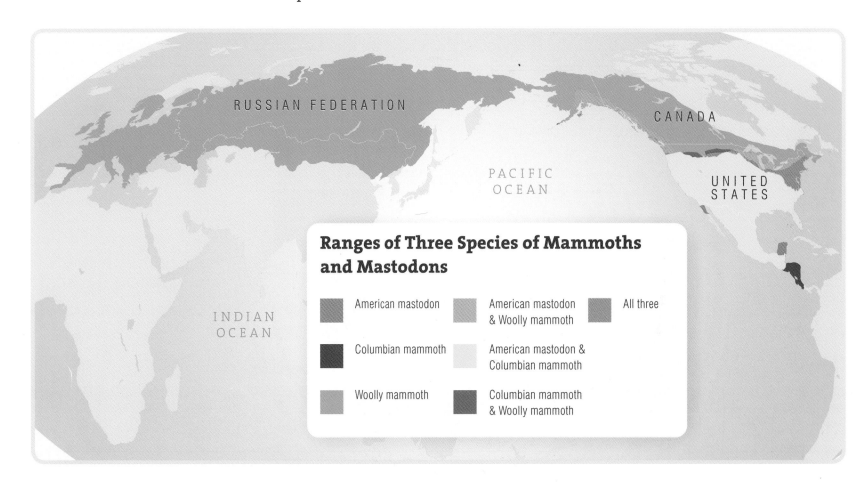

Ranges of Three Species of Mammoths and Mastodons

- American mastodon
- American mastodon & Woolly mammoth
- All three
- Columbian mammoth
- American mastodon & Columbian mammoth
- Woolly mammoth
- Columbian mammoth & Woolly mammoth

▲ Mammoths and mastodons once thrived across vast areas of the globe. Although their ranges overlapped, each species was suited to a specific habitat.

The Mammoth Name Game

Most people would call any hairy elephant a woolly mammoth. To better understand these creatures of the past, imagine you are on a game show, sitting across from three ... well, hairy elephants.

The game show host points to Creature A, which has giant, curved tusks and surprisingly small ears for such a big animal. Fur from its sides hangs like a skirt to its knees. "This guy lived in a cold world with few trees. He gorged himself on grass, willow shrubs, and buttercups."

Creature B is larger, with bigger tusks but shorter fur and a longer tail. The host says, "This fellow wandered in a warmer climate past red-rock buttes as far south as modern-day Costa Rica. He chomped on grass, sagebrush, and fir needles."

Creature C has shorter legs and a longer, stockier body than the other two. He also has shorter fur than Creature A. The host comments, "He foraged in forests on swamp grass and tree bark."

UNPACKING THE TRUNK

Trunks are unique to mammoths, mastodons, and elephants and can do everything that a human hand can do—and then some. Their fingerlike tips caress calves and pick up objects as small as a dime. They are built of strong muscles that can lift heavy objects and lash out at enemies. They smell flowers and trumpet messages. Trunks can also be used as snorkels when swimming, or to suck up and squirt out water.

MEET THE PROBOSCIDEANS

The first proboscidean, called *Moeritherium*, lived in swamps 50 million years ago. This animal looked like a large pig with a long snout and small tusks. Over millions of years, proboscideans grew larger and developed trunks. Their tusks evolved into a variety of shapes and sizes.

Three proboscidean species remain today. Asian elephants and African forest elephants munch on leaves and bark in rain forests. African savanna elephants ramble on plains and through woodlands to eat grass during the rainy season, and then they gnaw on bark in the dry season. All of today's elephants have sparse coats. Long tails and giant ears give elephants large areas of skin that allow heat to escape their bodies.

The host grins at you. "To be a bona fide Mammoth Maniac, answer these questions:

1. Are all these creatures real?

2. Are they all woolly mammoths?

3. Which is the ancestor of modern-day elephants?"

Ticktock, ticktock. BUZZZZ. Time's up!

The correct answers, in order, are:

1. Yes, each creature did exist.
2. Creature A is a woolly mammoth, Creature B is a Columbian mammoth, and Creature C is an American mastodon.
3. Trick question! Elephants, mammoths, and mastodons are cousins; none descended from the others. Before mammoths and mastodons went extinct, they shared the Earth with elephants.

A closer look reveals how each animal on our game show was adapted to thrive in its specific habitat. Woolly mammoths ranged mostly across frigid plains. Their coats had a fine, dense layer that acted like long underwear, a longer middle layer, and an outer layer that worked like a parka. Columbian mammoths and American mastodons had shorter fur so they wouldn't overheat in milder climates.

A smaller body size allowed woolly mammoths to get by with less food than their southern cousins. Plentiful food in warmer climates helped Columbian mammoths grow taller and heavier than woolly mammoths. Ample food also allowed American mastodons to bulk up, although they were shorter than the other two species.

▲ The woolly mammoth tooth (left) has many sharp ridges for grinding grass. The mastodon tooth (right) has a few large bumps for crushing tree bark, twigs, and leaves.

Also, each animal's teeth were suited to its favorite foods. Woolly mammoth molars had up to 26 pairs of ridges to grind grass, grass, and more grass. Columbian mammoths had fewer ridges, spaced farther apart because their diet included a wider variety of plants in addition to grass. American mastodon molars had a few rounded domes for crushing the leaves, twigs, and bark found in their woodland homes.

These animals are part of a group called proboscideans, a name that comes from the Latin word for *nose*. Over time the proboscidean family tree has had at least 165 different species. Dr. Fisher says such variety in a group of large animals is incredible because the members of each species must find a way to fill their vast bellies. (Columbian mammoths ate up to 500 pounds of food each day. That would be like eating more than 500 cans of green beans . . . every day.)

For millions of years, proboscideans wandered across every continent except Antarctica and Australia. They made homes in rain forests, prairies, woodlands, and tundra. Now only elephants remain. If so many proboscideans succeeded in so many places for so long, then why has this mighty group of animals almost disappeared? Is it possible to save the elephants that are left?

Present

▲ African elephant, *Loxodonta africana*, 10–11 feet tall, 4–6 tons, 5 million years ago to present

▲ Columbian mammoth, *Mammuthus columbi*, 13 feet tall, 10 tons, 100,000–10,000 years ago

5 million years

Proboscidean Family Tree

10 million years

20 million years

30 million years

▶ *Moeritherium*, 2.5 feet tall, around 50 million years ago

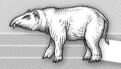

50 million years

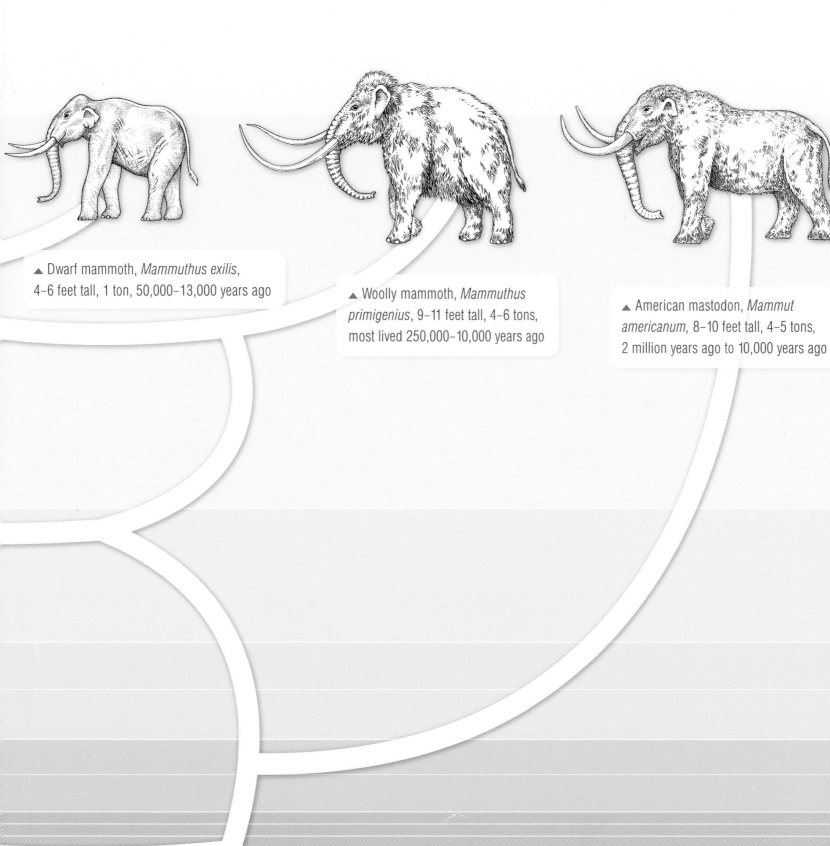

▲ Dwarf mammoth, *Mammuthus exilis*, 4–6 feet tall, 1 ton, 50,000–13,000 years ago

▲ Woolly mammoth, *Mammuthus primigenius*, 9–11 feet tall, 4–6 tons, most lived 250,000–10,000 years ago

▲ American mastodon, *Mammut americanum,* 8–10 feet tall, 4–5 tons, 2 million years ago to 10,000 years ago

▲ The inside of a mammoth tusk looks like a stack of ice-cream cones. Tusks grow from the base and push outward, so the oldest layers (formed when the animal was young) are at the tip.

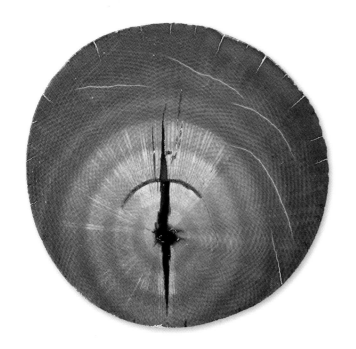

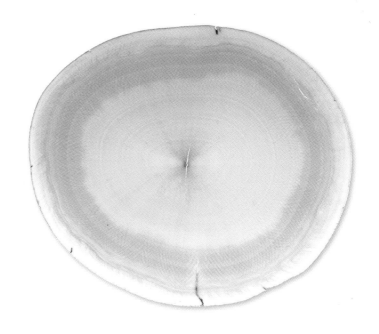

Reading Tales in the Tusks

Dr. Fisher believes mammoth and mastodon tusks, which are a special kind of teeth, hold clues about why these animals went extinct. About 30 years ago, Dr. Fisher noticed a series of dark and light lines on the inside of a mastodon tusk that had cracked open. In a flash of recognition, Dr. Fisher experienced the kind of "Aha!" moment that lasts a lifetime. The lines must be layers of tusk material, which grow throughout the mastodon's life—just like the layers of new wood that create growth rings in trees. Tree rings are wider when a tree lived through a favorable growing season, and narrower when the tree suffered, perhaps due to drought or disease. Could scientists analyze tusk layers the same way they

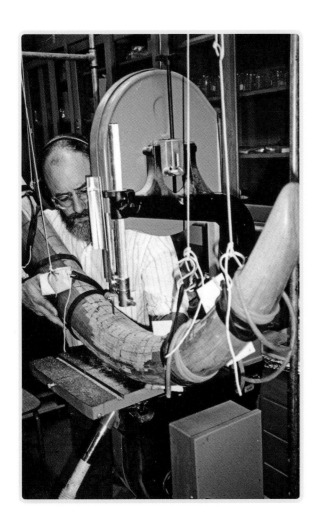

▲ Dr. Fisher patiently and carefully saws an adult mastodon tusk in half.

examine tree rings? Dr. Fisher's face tingled as he realized how this one discovery could lead to many more. "It was like finding an open book, filled with answers to our questions about mastodons—if only we knew how to read it."

Dr. Fisher used a precision saw, one with diamond dust embedded in the blade, to trim thin slices of tusk. He polished and polished each slice until light shone through. Under a microscope, the slices revealed even more than he expected. Trees usually add a new growth ring every year. Mammoths and mastodons, however, added a new layer of tooth tissue, called dentin, to their tusks every *day*. The faster the dentin grew, the lighter the color of the tusk's growth ring. The rings formed patterns that followed daily, weekly, seasonal, and yearly cycles. This amount of data is "mind-boggling," Dr. Fisher says. "Not many animals have such a complete record of their lives, even among living animals."

Until the baby mammoth Lyuba, none of the tusks Dr. Fisher examined were attached to a body. Lyuba gave Dr. Fisher a unique chance to compare what he can learn from an animal's tusks to the information gathered from the rest of its body. In the first year after Lyuba's discovery, scientists explored her guts with a tiny camera, viewed her cells under a microscope, and used a CT scanner to take detailed pictures of her insides. They concluded that Lyuba was fit as a fiddle before she choked on mud at one month old. The layers in Lyuba's tiny tusks match the other evidence of good health. This confirmed Dr. Fisher's theory that tusks offer a snapshot of an animal's overall well-being. He hopes to study lots of tusks to document how healthy mammoths and mastodons were when their species went extinct.

When Dr. Fisher began his career, scientists knew some of what these animals ate, but not how long they lived, or much else about their lives. Along with Lyuba and other fossil finds, Dr. Fisher's tusk research is filling in the gaps. Patterns in tusk rings can reveal how old a mammoth was when it died and whether it died in the winter or summer. Tusks mark when females gave birth and show scars of mating battles among males. Dr. Fisher can even measure the amount of various chemicals trapped in each dentin growth layer to find out what kinds of food an animal was eating and what the local climate was like when the animal was alive.

At last scientists have enough information about mammoths and mastodons to paint a portrait of daily life for these bygone beasts. Understanding how they lived is an important step toward understanding how they died. Understanding how they died is an important step toward preventing elephants from meeting the same fate.

◀ Dr. Fisher (left) removes Lyuba's baby tusk—that tiny thing at the end of the tweezers.

Piecing Together Mammoth Reality

Episode 1: Baby Lyuba

Pretend you are filming a new television documentary. For this episode, travel by time machine 40,000 years into the past to visit a family of woolly mammoths traveling across Asia. Unpack your camera and focus a telephoto lens on the smallest baby (mammoth babies are called calves).

While her mother and aunts graze on grass and willow shrubs, three-week-old Lyuba watches other calves play tag. A cousin pokes Lyuba with her trunk and then lies down to play King-of-the-Mountain, mammoth-style. Lyuba struggles to climb the cousin's back. Just as she is about to succeed, the cousin stands and Lyuba slips. THUMP! Lyuba lifts her trunk, opens her mouth . . . and squeals with delight. The next time she falls, her foot crashes into something cold and wet. The cousin has accidentally lain too close to the river. Lyuba squeaks for help. Her watchful mother and aunts pull her onto solid ground, murmuring comfort and checking her over with the tips of their trunks.

Suddenly, Lyuba's grandmother, the family leader, bellows an alarm. Calves huddle while adults surround them. A saber-toothed cat snarls and skulks closer. The attacker spies an opening and lunges at Lyuba. THUD! One of Lyuba's towering aunts swipes with a sturdy tusk and tosses the predator into the air. The defeated cat lands with a yowl of rage and limps off.

That's a wrap. Pack up the camera and skedaddle before the saber-tooth comes after you!

OPPOSITE A family of woolly mammoths fends off a hungry saber-toothed cat, which is trying to feed cubs of her own.

▶ When danger looms, female elephants form a defensive circle around their young. Fossils suggest that mammoths did the same.

OPPOSITE Elephants greet friends by twining trunks. Mammoths did, too, according to the paintings made 15,000 to 20,000 years ago in the Rouffignac Cave in France.

Behind the Scenes of Episode 1

Too bad we can't travel back in time to watch mammoth calves romp. Instead, we create these vivid scenes by examining living elephants as context for studying the remains of mammoths and mastodons. Wherever the evidence matches up, it is reasonable to suppose that mammoths and elephants behaved in similar ways.

Let's start with the skeletons of 15 Columbian mammoths that died in what is now Texas. These animals were all females and calves who died together. Their skeletons lay in a circle, with calves in the center and adults on the outside. Luckily, scientists can look to elephants to make sense of this graveyard. Young elephants grow up in families of adult females, usually led by the eldest in the group. (Adult males wander alone or in twos or threes.) If a herd is threatened, mothers, aunts, and grandmothers form a living fortress around the calves. Danger stays out while calves stay in—unless the danger is a flash flood or mudslide, which is how scientists believe the Texas group died all together. Seeing similar social patterns in living elephants helps us understand the fossil record of mammoths.

DO THESE ELEPHANTS AND MAMMOTHS SEEM ALMOST HUMAN?

"Elephants portray their intelligence and emotions in ways that we recognize in ourselves," says Dr. Jacqueline Codron, who studies wild elephants in South Africa. As a result, scientists have observed surprising similarities between elephant and human societies.

Elephants recognize each other as individuals and greet family and friends by embracing their trunks. They help fallen elephants get back on their feet. They even stand vigil by a dead family member for days, and later revisit the site to stroke a loved one's bones with their trunks. Evidence from mammoths and mastodons suggests they shared many of these behaviors with elephants.

The tusk analysis done by Dr. Fisher and his graduate students tells us that mammoth calves drank milk from their mothers for up to six years. Compared to other animals, this is a long childhood. Modern elephants, which nurse their babies for an average of five years, spend longer raising their calves than any other animals except humans and a few species of whales. Scientists have watched young elephants play rough-and-tumble and learn the rules of society from their elders. Baby mammoths and mastodons probably did the same. A game of chase between two young mammoths is even recorded in muddy footprints that hardened into rock in Canada.

Episode 2: Teen Bull in Trouble

Let's trek to the plains of North America. Focus the camera on that 13-year-old Columbian mammoth knocking about by himself.

> *All around, remnants of snow are melting to reveal last year's stringy grass. Up ahead, however, the young bull spies a pond amid what looks like a summer garden in bloom. With a giddyap, our mammoth bellies up to the buffet. Mmmm. The sage and mustard greens are crunchy. The bank is more slippery than he expected, and he lurches into the pond. The water is warm. The look on his face says, "Ah. This is the life."*
>
> *After eating and drinking his fill, the mammoth hoists a leg onto the bank. SPLASH! His body rocks off-kilter as the foot plunges back into the water. Uh-oh. The steep slope that brought him slip-sliding into this pond makes it impossible to climb out.*

You can turn the camera off. He won't make it out alive.

▲ The bank of this sinkhole is too steep for the young Columbian mammoth to climb out, even with help from a friend.

▶ Dramatic tusks can make mammoth skulls easy to spot at Hot Springs, South Dakota. The sinkhole also snared prairie dogs, wolves, giant camels, and a variety of other animals.

OPPOSITE Dr. Larry Agenbroad excavates a mammoth skeleton in Hot Springs. A planned housing development for this site was canceled, and a museum was built instead.

Behind the Scenes of Episode 2

In Hot Springs, South Dakota, scientists have unearthed the bones of 55 Columbian mammoths. The animals were trapped 30,000 years ago in a sinkhole where warm water bubbled from the ground all year. Eventually the sinkhole filled with mud, which blanketed the bones. This site was discovered in 1974 when bulldozers cleared land to build houses. Someone stubbed their toe on a mammoth tooth, and scientists have been excavating ever since.

The placement of bones at Hot Springs tells scientists these mammoths died one at a time, over the course of 300 to 700 years. All the skeletons are male. Almost all died between the ages of 11 and 29. (Scientists estimate mammoths lived about 60 years.) What lured these young bulls to their deaths?

Dr. Larry Agenbroad has studied the Hot Springs mammoths since their discovery. He explains: "When you look at elephant society, these years are when junior gets kicked out of the family. He's wandering around, mostly alone." During this long adolescence, when the elephants are almost grown up but not quite, the bulls spar (trade blows with their tusks) to test strength and learn skills that will one day attract mates. Alone in the world for the first time, without the guidance of their wise mothers and aunts, they also goof off. Dr. Agenbroad once witnessed a young elephant bull storm out of a forest, scatter zebras and birds from a water hole, and then charge into the distance—for no apparent reason. Sometimes such mischief leads to trouble. "It's not a big mind leap," Dr. Agenbroad says, to conclude that young mammoth bulls behaved the same.

Dr. Fisher's tusk research supports this theory. Most of the Hot Springs mammoths died in fall or early spring. Warm water would have coaxed plants along the sinkhole bank to sprout earlier, and stay green longer, than on the surrounding plains. The mammoths that died here came looking for an easy lunch. More mature mammoths had likely seen others get stuck and knew to avoid such traps. The younger bulls didn't recognize the danger in the slippery slope that sealed their fate. Even if a nearby herd responded to cries of distress, it is unlikely that a helping trunk could have pulled many victims back up the steep slope.

THE MINI-MAMMOTHS

Skeletons of dwarf mammoths that stood four to six feet tall have been found on islands near California. These animals descended from the Columbian mammoths living on the mainland. The mini-mammoths had mini-appetites, and so they could survive better on islands, which provide less room to graze.

Season Finale: Bulls Battle

Now visit an ancient forest in the Midwestern United States. Be sure to film from a safe distance.

Two mastodon bulls face off. Fluid oozes from glands in their cheeks. One bull brandishes his tusks. The other scoops up a log and tosses it at his foe. The ground trembles as they charge. Their heads crash and a thunderous crack echoes through the trees. The bulls lock tusks, and each tries to knock the other off its feet. One bull ducks his head to pull away. The other bull crashes rock-hard tusks onto the retreating shoulders. Ouch! That's got to hurt. The injured bull limps away, while the victor swaggers off to find a mate.

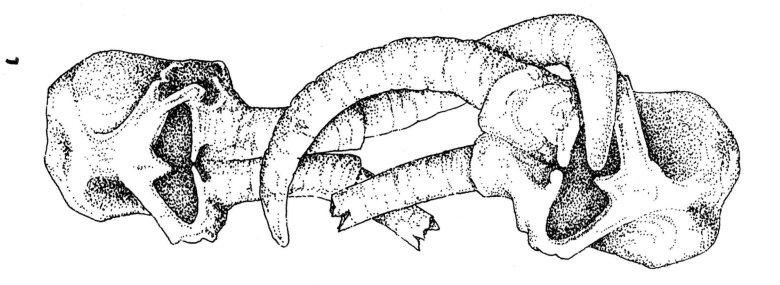

Behind the Scenes of the Season Finale

As you can see, these animals were not always gentle giants.

Mature elephant bulls spend about two months each year vying for mates. Scientists call this time *musth*. During musth, fluid streams out of gland openings on a bull's cheek. Deep, rumbling noises resonate from his throat. Females smell and hear musth bulls from a half mile away. They are attracted to bulls that have proven their strength—and sometimes these duels between males end in death.

Gland openings on the cheeks of a frozen mammoth head tell us they experienced musth, too. Broken ribs and shoulder blades as well as punctured skulls offer ample evidence of brawling. Dr. Fisher used computer animation to model how mastodons may have maneuvered their tusks to stab through 20 inches of muscle to deliver the fatal wounds he found in the cheekbones of some male skulls. "They dipped their heads down," he explains, "and then stepped forward while rearing up with great force. It was like two garbage trucks ramming one another with prongs sticking out in front."

▲ Drawn from a fossil found in Nebraska, this illustration shows how a battle ended poorly for two Columbian mammoths, which could not untangle their tusks.

OPPOSITE Mastodon bulls battle in a Midwestern woodland. Females were most attracted to mates who won these tests of strength.

▲ Ancient people likely worked together to hunt this dangerous prey. In Arizona, eight spear points were found wedged between the bones of a single adult mammoth.

Prehistoric People and Mammoths

Now that you've seen these creatures in action, have you got the guts to take one on? Consider your strategy carefully. A young mammoth would put up less of a fight, but you might attract the wrath of a whole herd. A male mammoth is likely to travel alone, but be no less deadly. Maybe you should hunt something safer, like a rabbit. Keep in mind that you'll need more than 1,000 arctic hares to equal the meat on one woolly mammoth.

Some scientists question whether enough evidence exists to know if humans regularly hunted mammoths. Some bones bear marks from where people sliced meat off with stone knives. However, ancient peoples could have scavenged animals that were already dead. Doubters wonder if people could have used up enough of the meat from a mammoth, before it rotted, to make such a dangerous hunt worthwhile.

▲ More than 150 mammoths lumber across the walls of Rouffignac Cave in France. They were painted 15,000 to 20,000 years ago.

▲ Stacked jawbones form walls, while tusks arch to create the doorway of this modern copy of a mammoth bone hut.

Dr. Fisher and other scientists believe hunters banded together to catch mammoths and mastodons just as they have done with elephants. For evidence, researchers point to a dozen mammoth skeletons that have been found with spear points lodged between their bones. Classic hunting tricks could have reduced the risk to attackers. In England, a group of 20 mammoth skeletons was found at the base of a cliff, as if these animals had been herded into a stampede to their deaths. Cave paintings in France suggest hunters may have dug pitfalls, or holes, to trap mammoths, which couldn't climb out since their legs would be pinned beneath them.

Successful hunters would have had enough meat to feed a group of 25 people for about a month. Dr. Fisher believes he has discovered what prehistoric peoples used as refrigerators. Several mastodon finds in bogs and ponds have been only partial skeletons. These bones showed signs of being butchered and seemed to have been anchored in the water.

When a draft horse on a nearby farm died of old age, Dr. Fisher began an experiment. He used stone tools to butcher the horse. Without using any plastic wrap or aluminum foil, he submerged the raw meat into a shallow Michigan pond in February. Each week he sliced off a steak to eat. He tried several techniques for open-fire cooking and decided the best was to lay the steak directly on the hot coals. "You take it out of the fire," he says, "hit it a few times to knock the ashes off, and bite."

When the pond thawed in the spring, the meat floated to the surface of the water. Then Dr. Fisher understood the importance of anchoring the meat away from the shore. "If you can keep it bobbing out in the middle of the pond, scavengers will stay away," he says. Dr. Fisher ate the last of his pond-stored steaks at a Fourth of July barbecue. Although the meat was safe to eat, Dr. Fisher says it did taste "less fresh" over time. Of course, you shouldn't try such an experiment on your own. Dr. Fisher tested the meat for harmful bacteria throughout his research.

People valued mammoths for other reasons, too. On the arctic plains of Russia, where trees were in short supply, some prehistoric people relied on mammoth skeletons to provide materials for shelter. Seventy huts have been found that were built of mammoth bones more than 18,000 years ago. Twenty-five skulls form a large circle as the base of one shelter, which was constructed from about 385 bones total. Scientists believe people covered these structures in animal skins—perhaps also from mammoths—to block wind and cold.

Mammoths also gave early peoples inspiration. After horses and bison, mammoths are the animal most frequently painted on cave walls. Ancient people also carved mammoths from ivory and bone. Scientists don't know the meaning of this art. Elephants have long been revered as symbols of strength and wisdom, and perhaps people once honored mammoths and mastodons in the same way.

Then one day, the mammoths and mastodons were gone.

▶ About 25,000 years ago, a teenage boy may have stenciled his hand on the wall of Pech Merle Cave in France.

KID CAVE ARTISTS

Thousands of years ago, someone pressed their fingers into soft clay to carve patterns into cave walls and ceilings. Today we call these marks finger flutings. After measuring the grooves in Rouffignac Cave in France, scientists believe many of them to be the work of children ages two to five years old, who were seated on the shoulders of grown-ups.

Measurements of other cave art suggest that teenage boys made many of the stenciled handprints found on the walls of the Chauvet-Pont-d'Arc Cave in France and at least 30 other European caves.

Scientists don't know if these artworks were important rituals or just fun doodles.

▶ Ancient Greeks mistook mammoth bones to be the bones of a Cyclops—a giant with one eye in the middle of his forehead.

OPPOSITE The first known American mastodon was discovered on a New York farm in 1801. Excavating mammoths and mastodons can still be muddy work today.

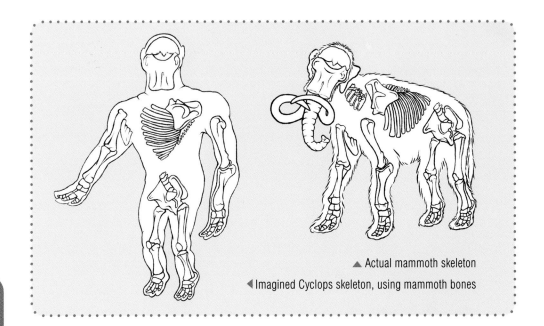

▲ Actual mammoth skeleton

◀ Imagined Cyclops skeleton, using mammoth bones

TEENS EXCAVATE A MASTODON

In 2007, 15-year-old Bennet spent two weeks searching for an ancient mastodon at the edge of a muddy Illinois marsh. Wielding a garden trowel, he found 15 shards of tusk, all less than three inches long.

Bennet was part of a summer camp organized by The Field Museum in Chicago and the Forest Preserve District of DuPage County. He now knows that real science isn't like in the movies: "I thought the mastodon would be right there, ready to be dug up."

Every piece of prehistory, Bennet says, was worth the effort.

Following the Mammoth Trail

People have stumbled over mammoth and mastodon remains for thousands of years. Ancient Greeks believed these were the bones of giants. Arctic peoples thought they were oversized, evil moles that died when exposed to sunlight. President Thomas Jefferson assumed mastodon skeletons came from rare elephants hiding in American forests. He felt such mighty beasts would prove our young nation to be a mighty land. Instead, in 1806, the American mastodon became the first animal ever to be declared extinct. (Before then, people thought the animals on Earth never changed.)

Fast-forward to today, when some people talk about bringing mammoths back to life. Thanks to frozen cells from finds like Lyuba, scientists can estimate that the genes of mammoths and

elephants are 99.4 percent the same. Science is still a long way, however, from cloning a woolly mammoth to trundle across the plains. Even if scientists had all the data and technology needed, they don't have any live mammoth cells. They would have to insert mammoth genes into elephant cells. "The resulting animal would be part mammoth and part elephant," Dr. Fisher explains. "You couldn't be sure that the animal looked or behaved like a real mammoth."

A more urgent challenge is figuring out what caused mammoths and mastodons to go extinct.

Map labels:
RUSSIAN FEDERATION

ARCTIC OCEAN

EUROPE

PACIFIC OCEAN

CANADA

ATLANTIC OCEAN

UNITED STATES

From the Ice Age to Today

☐ Polar cap and continental ice sheets today

▨ Continental ice sheets 21,000 years ago

The Mammoth Mystery

Imagine if Africa had three-quarters of its large animals zapped away. No more elephants, no more giraffes, no more rhinos. That happened on other continents 10,000 years ago. Seventy percent of the mammals weighing more than 100 pounds went extinct. In North America, that meant no more mammoths, giant camels, or giant beavers. If scientists could puzzle out

▲ Glaciers reached the farthest around 21,000 years ago. By about 12,000 years ago, glaciers had shrunk almost to their modern locations.

OPPOSITE Understanding what wiped out mammoths and mastodons around 10,000 years ago could help us save the wild elephants, buffalo, and other mega-mammals that are threatened today the world over.

▶ About 11,000 years ago, the Clovis people who lived in North America used tools made of stone, antler, and bone to sharpen the edges of this deadly spear point.

▲ Scientists have experimented with making and using replicas of Ice Age weapons. A weapon like this replica could have penetrated deep into the rib cage of a mammoth, even if thrown from 65 feet away.

why mammoths and mastodons went extinct, they might also explain the loss of other mega-mammals—and help save those that are left today.

Some scientists blame climate change. Glaciers, which are massive buildups of ice, were at their largest during some of the mammoths' reign. This is why the era is sometimes called the Ice Age. Around 14,000 years ago, the Earth had a heat wave. Glaciers shrank until they covered only the polar caps. Prairies that once were like the landscape of Edmonton, Canada (average high in June of 70°F, or 21°C), changed to be more like the landscape of Missoula, Montana (average high in June of 73°F, or 23°C). In some areas, the change was greater. Even a few degrees' difference can be enough to change what trees and grasses can grow, altering what is available for mammoths and other large animals to eat.

◄ This carving of a mammoth, made from a reindeer antler 16,500 years ago, is an important tool called an atlatl (*aht-laht-l*). Although the mammoth's head and trunk bend down to its feet, its tusks outline a handle for gripping. Spears hooked onto the pointy tail. The atlatl extended the reach of a hunter's arm to add power to his throw.

Critics of this theory say that if climate change was dramatic enough to kill off mega-mammals, it should have hurt smaller species, too. Also, mammoths and mastodons had survived warm-ups before. Dr. Fisher's tusk research actually shows that mammoths and mastodons ate well amid the climate change.

Some scientists believe humans hunted mammoths and mastodons to extinction. These animals usually vanished from an area after large groups of humans arrived. Even if every family killed just one mammoth a year for its own survival, this would mean a higher death rate than before people came. "Over thousands of years, this takes a toll," Dr. Fisher says. "People probably didn't realize the mammoths were dying out until they went to hunt and had trouble finding them."

Understanding the impact of such individual actions is hard, even in the present. "It's easy to think it won't matter if we take one more," Dr. Fisher says. "It does matter because it's one more,

THE LAST MAMMOTHS

A small group of woolly mammoths was still roaming around until about 3,900 years ago—about the time ancient Egyptians were building the last great pyramids. The skeletons of these mammoths were found on a Russian island in the Arctic Ocean. Some scientists suspect these woolly mammoths survived so long because humans had not yet reached these islands.

and then one more again." The mass killing of elephants in the 1800s for their ivory demonstrates Dr. Fisher's point. "There were so many elephants in Africa that people would have laughed if you said that they would soon be close to extinct. Then people saw the numbers cut in half in just decades."

The immense size of mammoths made them vulnerable to habitat loss. They needed vast areas to graze. Both climate change and hunting could have limited them to small pockets of safe habitat. Elephants face similar challenges today as their habitat is squeezed between roads and farms.

Large animals are also slow reproducers. Like elephants, mammoths gave birth to only one calf at a time. Based on Dr. Fisher's tusk research, females began giving birth around age 12 and gave birth about every four years. Any increase in the death rate would have reduced mammoth herds quickly. Low population numbers put species at risk: "What would have been a small threat becomes a large threat," Dr. Fisher says.

Climate change and hunting are the two leading theories to explain the mega-loss of mega-mammals, although some scientists wonder if a virus or a comet's collision with the Earth may be to blame. Dr. Fisher is eager to examine more tusks, plus fossil bones and specimens like Lyuba. He will follow the clues wherever they lead. "Without some willingness to question what we know today," he says, "we're never going to look at the world differently from what we were taught." Solving this mystery could change how we think about mammoths and elephants. It could even change how we see the relationship between humans and other animals.

▲ The survival of elephants is currently threatened by ivory poaching and habitat loss. Elephants are the last remaining members of the once-mighty proboscidean clan that included mammoths and mastodons.

Saving the Elephants

Dr. Jacqueline Codron is one of the first scientists to use tusk analysis to help elephants today.

A few years ago, something was destroying the trees that kudu, giraffes, and other animals needed to survive at Kruger National Park in South Africa. Elephants were the largest animals around, so they were an easy scapegoat. Park managers considered killing some elephants to keep the ecosystem in balance. Dr. Codron wondered if elephants were really the culprits.

If the elephants were eating trees, evidence would show up in the chemical makeup of their dung and tail hairs. Dr. Codron started her investigation there. Then she used Dr. Fisher's techniques for tusk analysis to track the diets of park elephants during the past 100 years. She made a surprising discovery.

Elephants eat fewer trees in the park now than they did 100 years ago. "The elephants seem to eat more trees during stressful times," Dr. Codron explains, "for example during droughts, or when they face sudden changes to their environment." Although elephants are not completely off the hook for the tree loss, park managers and scientists are searching for other explanations and solutions that don't require killing elephants.

▲ Dr. Jacqueline Codron analyzes elephant tusks to look for patterns in the animals' diet over time.

▶ Now that the baby mammoth Lyuba is no longer frozen, her body could decay. After taking tissue samples for further study, scientists will dip Lyuba's body in a chemical preservative and allow it to dry out.

◀ A woolly mammoth skeleton. Who knows what exciting discoveries the future holds when we study the remains of the past?

Dr. Fisher says this success is just the start of how a technique that was developed by studying mammoths and mastodons can help elephants. Every year research methods grow and new discoveries are made. Dr. Fisher expects that in 20 years a new generation of scientists will exclaim "Aha!" while examining a tusk or the incredible specimen of Lyuba. With hard work and luck, we might unravel the secrets of these animals from the past—and prevent elephants from following in their footsteps.

And so a new generation—maybe you!—will write the next chapter in the mammoth story.

IF THEY ALL LIVED AT THE SAME TIME, WHY DIDN'T THE ELEPHANTS GO EXTINCT ALONG WITH MAMMOTHS AND MASTODONS?

Answer: Scientists don't know. Some think elephants lived in dense jungles and had less contact with humans. Others say elephants were targeted less because people could hunt a wider variety of large animals in those habitats, such as rhinos, hippos, zebras, and antelope.

Glossary

Cloning: The process of creating an exact copy of a life-form from its genetic material.

Dinosaurs: A group of reptiles that included the largest animals ever to live on land and that died out 65 million years ago.

Evidence: Information that helps to form or prove a conclusion.

Fossil: Any remains of a plant or animal that have been preserved over time. Frozen mammoth parts count as fossils, even though they have not been transformed into rock.

Fossil record: All fossils and the information that can be gathered by looking at where and how fossils appear.

Gene: The basic unit of heredity. All plants and animals pass traits to their offspring through genes.

Glacier: A large mass of ice that moves slowly across land. Glaciers form when layers of snow build up over years.

Habitat: The natural environment where an animal or plant lives.

Ice Age: Technically, we live in an ice age now because glaciers cover the Earth's poles. Most often this term refers to a time more than 10,000 years ago, when glaciers also covered what is now Greenland, Canada, parts of the northern United States, and parts of northern Europe.

Mammals: A group of animals whose bodies are generally covered with hair and that give birth to live young, which mothers feed with milk.

Nomadic: Describes people who move from place to place rather than living in one place all year. Their travels follow seasonal cycles that affect food, water, and grazing land.

Paleontologist: A scientist who studies fossils of plants and animals from prehistoric times.

Prehistoric: From the time before humans began recording history.

Proboscidea: A group of mammals that includes mammoths, mastodons, and elephants. Members of this group have tusks and trunks.

Select References

Interviews

All the quotations that appear in this book are from interviews with Dr. Daniel Fisher, Dr. Lawrence Agenbroad, and Dr. Jacqueline Codron, which were conducted by the author from July through December 2008.

Books

Agenbroad, Larry D., and Lisa Nelson. *Mammoths: Ice Age Giants*. Minneapolis: Lerner Publications Co., 2002.

Giblin, James Cross. *The Mystery of the Mammoth Bones*. New York: HarperCollins Publishers, 1999.

Lister, Adrian, and Paul Bahn. *Mammoths: Giants of the Ice Age*. London: Frances Lincoln Limited Publisher, 2007.

Image credits

Index

Acknowledgments

This book has been published in conjunction with the exhibition *Mammoths and Mastodons: Titans of the Ice Age*, organized by The Field Museum, Chicago.

The author would like to thank those who contributed their passion and expertise to the creation of this book. Dr. Daniel Fisher at the University of Michigan; Dr. Lawrence Agenbroad at the Mammoth Site of Hot Springs, South Dakota; and Dr. Jacqueline Codron generously shared scientific expertise. Franck Mercurio, Tom Skwerski, Todd Tubutis, and David Quednau at The Field Museum provided valuable information and support. Photo researcher Deborah Van Kirk and artist Velizar Simeonovski gathered and created powerful images. Claire Rudolf Murphy, on faculty at Hamline University, helped shape the research into a story early on, and editor Howard Reeves at Abrams Books for Young Readers polished the text with clarity and finesse.

**To my mom, who has inspired me
and hundreds of other children
to explore the world through science.**

—C. B.

Library of Congress Cataloging-in-Publication Data

Bardoe, Cheryl, 1971–
Mammoths and mastodons : titans of the Ice Age / by Cheryl Bardoe.
p. cm.
"Published in conjunction with the Field Museum of Chicago."
ISBN 978-0-8109-8413-4 (Harry N. Abrams)
1. Mammoths—Juvenile literature. 2. Mastodons—Juvenile literature. 3. Paleontology—Pleistocene—Juvenile literature. I. Title.
QE882.P8B37 2010
569'.67—dc22
2009022006

Text and color illustrations copyright © 2010 The Field Museum
Book design by Maria T. Middleton

Printed and bound in China
10 9 8 7 6 5

ABRAMS
THE ART OF BOOKS SINCE 1949
115 West 18th Street
New York, NY 10011
www.abramsbooks.com

The Field Museum